the WIZARD'S TALE

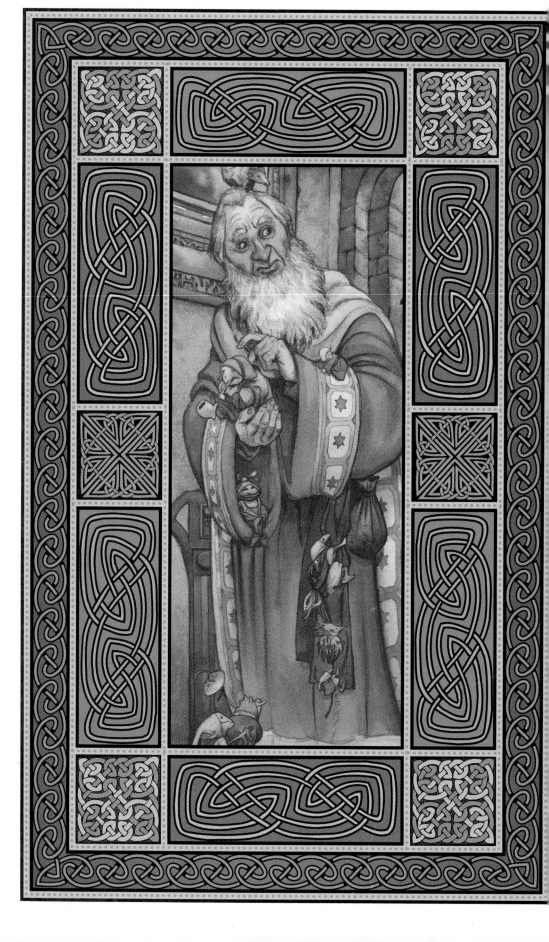

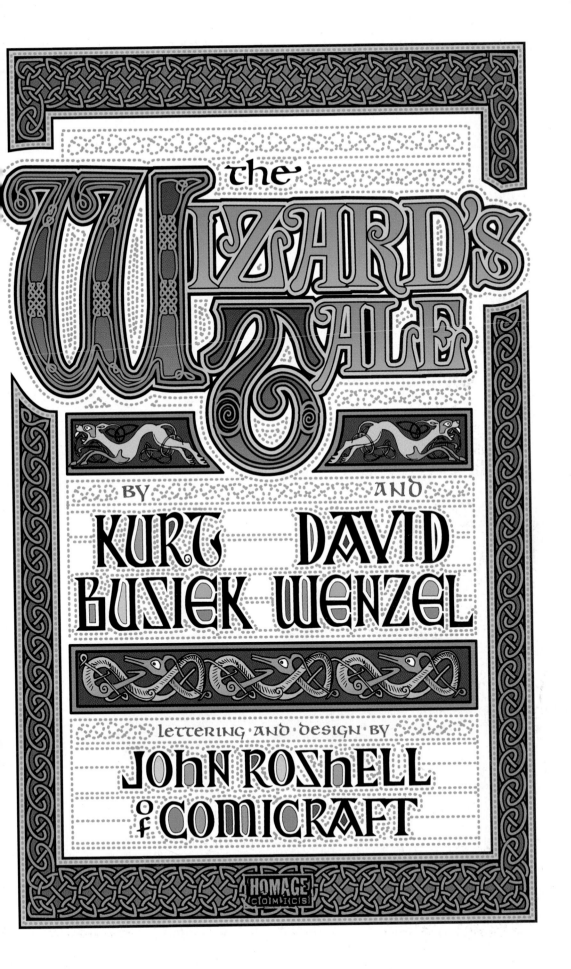

the WIZARD'S TALE

BY · AND

KURT BUSIEK · DAVID WENZEL

LETTERING · AND · DESIGN · BY

JOHN ROSHELL
OF COMICRAFT

HOMAGE COMICS

To James Thurber,
Edward Eager,
Jane Langton,
Lloyd Alexander,
Joan Aiken and all the
others who made my
childhood full of magic
— KURT

To the child in all of us —
especially Brendan and
Christopher, my buds.
— DAVID

For HOMAGE COMICS:

JIM   JEFF   JOE
LEE   MARIOTTE   COTRUPE
Publisher   Marketing   Manufacturing
            Director   Director

JOHN LAYMAN   SARAH DITZER
Assistant Editor   Traffic

For WILDSTORM PRODUCTIONS:
Hafid Boulanouar, Bonnie Bremner,
Ruth Castillo, Claudia Chong,
Jennifer Fenner, Erin Gering, Amie
Grenier, Tom Long, Bob Partridge,
Chris Provinzano, Rob Robbins,
Ed Roeder & Thom Sullivan

Bus
B&T 10/02 19.95
15.96

HAVE TO ADMIT

I find it somewhat surprising that high fantasy in comics hasn't had the same success as it has in prose.

(Quick definition here: by high fantasy I mean Tolkienesque quest epics set in a secondary world where magic works, the woods are riddled with elves, dwarves are busy hammering out swords and rings deep underground, wizards are looking suitably grim and mysterious as they utter enigmatic advice, etc.)

One would think that the medium would lend itself to such stories far more readily than, say, the film industry does. For one thing, the special effects budget would be minimal since it costs no more to have an artist draw an elf, a dwarf, a dragon, a castle, than it does to draw a human being, a superhero, a scantily-clad "bad girl" Rambo clone.

But we haven't seen the huge bestseller success of Terry Brooks, David Eddings or Robert Jordan repeated in the comics field. Elfquest probably comes closest although, for all its elves and the quest in its title, it's always struck me as having a much closer connection to sword & sorcery than it does high fantasy.

I t doesn't make much sense.

It can't be because the readers of one aren't aware of the other. Both comics and fantasy are considered literary underdogs, and are often happily embraced by the same audience, yet a commercially successful creative crossover between the two simply hasn't appeared to date.

The Wizard's Tale might well change that — or at least open the door to that change because, to be fair, it appears more related to a sub-genre of high fantasy dealing with humour (Terry Pratchett's novels might be the best prose example) in the same way that Elfquest appears to owe as much to Robert E. Howard as it does Tolkien.

For comic book touchstones, what comes immediately to my mind are the old Carl Barks Donald Duck strips and the French Tintin books, the former for its wonderful mix of solid plotting, improbable scenarios and good-natured humour, the latter for its sensibility and unabashed joy of adventure.

B UT ENOUGH of my trying to fit The Wizard's Tale into some particular slot, or taking up space here wondering aloud why this sort of a story hasn't been a great commercial success before. What's more important is how well The Wizard's Tale works in its own right, and that it does wonderfully. I'm not really surprised, though, considering the quality of the talent involved in the project.

Kurt Busiek is the visionary writer who brought us the Marvels series that subsequently spawned a whole subgenre of superhero comics in which the superhero phenomena is examined from the outside — from the viewpoint of the ordinary lay person. He came to Marvels with a solid history of the superhero already under his belt, having scripted various issues of The Justice League of America, Wonder Woman, Spectacular Spider-Man and the like, and continues to work in the genre with Untold Tales of Spider-Man for Marvel Comics and his own Astro City, all of which prove he has just as good a take on writing superheroes from their own point of view.

But fantasy has always held a great interest for Busiek. As far back as his college years he was working on plots for children's books. At one point, inspired by the writing of James Thurber — most notably The 13 Clocks — Busiek worked up a plot about an evil wizard who simply didn't have the heart to be bad, and then promptly shelved it when he decided he didn't have Thurber's language skills.

Enter David Wenzel. If the cover and interior art of the book in which this introduction appears haven't already won you over, perhaps I should also mention his acclaimed work on The Hobbit, Fairy Tales of the Brothers Grimm and Kingdom of the Dwarfs. He's the perfect artist for a light-hearted fantasy tale, equally capable of depicting good-humoured protagonists and nasty villains, fantasy landscapes, dragons and of course those wonderfully sprite-like alchemites who mean so well but never quite manage to do a thing properly.

Jumping ahead from Busiek's aborted evil wizard story, we find Wenzel spending a day in traffic court, passing the time by doodling pictures of a gloomy-looking wizard surrounded by magical creatures. Curious about the character, he worked the wizard up a bit more, intending to do a children's book involving him. He and a writer friend worked on the book for awhile, but the story didn't gel, "largely," Busiek says, "because they made it about a little kid who gets drawn into a fantasy world and all the characters David liked got relegated to supporting roles of little significance."

So it, too, got shelved.

But something of those characters stayed with both author and artist and when a few years later the two were brought together by Cat Yronwode, then editor in chief at Eclipse Comics, The Wizard's Tale was born.

THE STORY is a delightful, slightly askew take on some of the principal tropes of high fantasy. Our hero is a wizard named Bafflerog Rumplewhisker who can't get his spells right — the difference here is he's an evil wizard whose botched spells do good rather than evil. He'd probably be more ashamed than he already is about it except that he doesn't really have the heart to see others treated badly, as witness his friendship with Gumpwort, an enchanted toad that everyone insists on calling a frog.

Then there's the quest in search of The Book of Worse, a collection of evil spells and power that the council of evil wizards need to bring a final darkness to Bafflerog's world. Bafflerog is sent off to find it, joined by Muddle, the third son of a wood-cutter, who's simply gung-ho to go on a quest, slay dragons and ogres, rescue princesses and generally do what needs to be done so that he can grow up to be a king, because that, he insists, is what happens to the third sons of wood-cutters, so long as they get to go on a quest.

To find out where the quest takes them and how it all works out, you'll need to read the story for yourself, but suffice it to say that Busiek takes us on a enjoyable romp that has as much fun with high fantasy as it does taking the genre seriously. And Wenzel's artwork is gorgeous throughout, a lovely mix of good comic book storytelling and book illustration. The full page panels on virtually every left hand page really let him cut loose with dramatic and highly detailed scenes, many of which wouldn't look out of place as posters in their own right.

But I don't need to tell you that. You only have to turn a couple of pages to find out for yourself. And then, you'll undoubtedly be rooting along with me that The Wizard's Tale will be the high fantasy comic book that breaks the mold and proves to be as much of a commercial success as some of its prose cousins.

It certainly deserves that wider audience.

Charles de Lint
Ottawa, autumn 1996

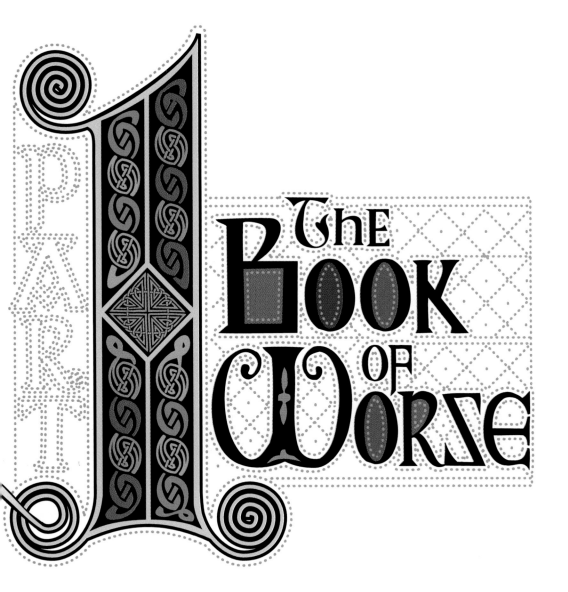

PART 1

THE BOOK OF WORSE

ALCHEMITES? *HAH!*
HOUSE-GOBLINS, MORE
LIKE! *WRECKLINGS!*
DISCOMBUMBLES!
MUCKERING
CLATTERFERING
FRETLETS!

I MAGIC
YOU UP TO AID
ME AND AND
YOU *FROLLIX*
ALL MY WORK!
YOU --

-- OH, NOW
DON'T CRY. IF
THERE'S ONE
THING I CAN'T
STAND, IT'S TO
SEE SOMETHING
I CREATED
CRY.

LOOK,
LOOK -- IT'S
STILL GOOD.
YOU DIDN'T
RUIN IT.

THAT'LL
TEACH
THEM.

WELL, IT WAS
ONLY A MOMENT,
GUMPWORT. THEY
CAN'T HAVE
DONE MUCH...

I
EXPECT IT'S
PERFECTLY
ALL
RIGHT...

WELL, I *HOPE*
IT'S ALL RIGHT --
THOSE WERE
THE LAST OF THE
FEWMETS, AND
IT'LL BE A FORT-
NIGHT BEFORE
THE NEXT
SHIPMENT
COMES...

...I'LL
GIVE IT
A TRY.

KRIK KRAK KROOM

HMM.

NOT EXACTLY WHAT I'D HOPED FOR, IS IT?

MAYBE IF YOU DIDN'T CAST YOUR SPELLS IN THE FORM OF LIMERICKS?

IT'S THE ONLY KIND OF RHYMING I'M ANY GOOD AT.

ARE THOSE VILLAGERS DOWN THERE? WHATEVER ARE THEY DOING?

THEY SEEM TO BE JUMPING FOR JOY.

BUT THEY'RE GETTING ALL WET!

THERE'S BEEN A DROUGHT RECENTLY -- THEY THOUGHT THEY'D LOSE THEIR CROPS AND STARVE.

NOW THEY WON'T THANKS TO YOU.

THEY'RE GRATEFUL. IT FIGURES. I ALWAYS MANAGE TO DO JUST EXACTLY THE WRONG THING.

OR THE TIME I TRIED FOR A HAIL OF LOCUSTS -- AND ENDED UP SHOWERING THEM WITH ROAST CHICKENS.

LOOK -- OVER THERE!

LIKE THE TIME I CAUSED AN EARTHQUAKE IN THE HILLS -- AND EXPOSED A VEIN OF GOLD.

WHAT NOW? IF IT'S THE ALCHEMITES AGAIN --

I HAVE FORGIVEN YOU *MUCH*, RUMPLEWHISKER, OUT OF RESPECT FOR YOUR *GREAT-GRANDFATHER'S* TRIUMPHS -- BUT YOU WOULD TRY THE PATIENCE OF AN *ANGEL!*

AND I *ASSURE* YOU -- NO ONE HAS EVER MISTAKEN ME FOR AN *ANGEL.*

N-NO, SIR.

SIR?

RRRMMMMMBBLL

S-SIR?

SIR, PLEASE DON'T --

CAN YOU *REMEMBER* THAT, RUMPLE-WHISKER?

Y-Y-Y-YES, S-S-SIR!

GOOD.

FOOF

KSSH

TIK

I THINK HE'S GONE.

ARE YOU ALL RIGHT, GUMPWORT?

"...AND AS THE LAST SUNBEAM RETREATED FROM THE POWER OF THE DARKSOME COUNCIL --

"-- THE PRINCESS WAS TURNED TO SUNLIGHT HERSELF, AND TRANSPORTED THROUGH TIME AND SPACE, TO A PLACE THE COUNCIL WOULD NEVER FIND HER."

THE LOST PRINCESS?

IT'S BEEN *RUMORED* SHE WAS CONNECTED TO THE DISAPPEARANCE OF THE BOOK, BUT...

Oh, THE *POOR GIRL!*

SENT AWAY FROM HER HOME AND FAMILY *FOREVER* -- KNOWING THAT THE FORCES OF EVIL WOULD NEVER STOP SEARCHING FOR HER!

WHY, IF I KNEW WHERE SHE WAS, I'D HAVE TO AFTER HER EVEN *NOW!*

INDEED.

YOU KNOW MUCH OF THE REST --

"-- HOW THE *FOOLISH* YOUNG WIZARD, OVERPROUD OF HIS SUCCESS, WAS EASILY CAPTURED BY GROATELAW...

"...AND TRANSFORMED INTO A CREATURE INCAPABLE OF WORKING MAGIC.

"THE
[SE]CRET REMAINED
[S]ECRET" -- *PFAH!*
[I] MEAN YOU WERE
[T]OO TOUGH TO
TALK!

AND DON'T
[GI]VE ME THIS
"*DIEHARDY*" STUFF.
[YOU'RE] A HERO AND
[I] KNOW IT -- UM,
THE FORCES
OF *LIGHT,*
ANYWAY.

AND
I'VE OFTEN
WONDERED
WHY YOU NEVER
TRIED TO ESCAPE.
SURELY YOU MUST
HAVE HAD PLENTY
OF *OPPOR-
TUNITIES...*

A
FEW.

BUT I
WAS WAITING
FOR SOME-
THING.

[A] MAGICAL
[MON]AD LIVES
[FA]R LONGER
[THAN] A HUMAN,
[SO] THE YEARS
[MEA]NT LITTLE
TO ME.

"I WAITED
[T]HROUGH THE
[T]IME OF YOUR
[G]RANDFATHER,
[C]RAGWIND..."

"...YOUR FATHER,
EARKWRATH..."

HOP,
TOAD
HOP!

YAH!
YAH!

KZAT

"...AND
FINALLY,
YOU."

YOU
KNOW, YOU
DON'T *LOOK*
LIKE A BASIL. YOU
LOOK LIKE A... A
GUMPWORT.

MAY I
CALL YOU
GUMPWORT?

"FFERENT" UTTING IT DLY, OLD FRIEND.

MOTHER SPENT HER DAYS LOST IN DREAMS -- AND I TOOK AFTER HER IN THAT, AT LEAST. FROM *FATHER*, ALL I GOT WAS THE RUMPLEWHISKER NOSE.

I ERTAINLY N'T GET HIS NACK FOR *ORCERY.*

"HE MUST HAVE DESPAIRED OF TEACHING ME MAGIC VERY EARLY ON..."

WOW! *NEAT!*

NO! NOT BEGONIAS -- BATS! *BATS!*

"STILL, HE NEVER GAVE UP. I'M SURE I DROVE HIM TO AN EARLY GRAVE.

"I REMEMBER THE FIRST TIME I TRIED TO CONJURE UP DRAGONS."

OOPS.

"WE FOUND NEWTS IN THE CASTLE FOR WEEKS THEREAFTER.

EVERY TIME HE'D SEE ONE, HE'D TURN RED AND HIS FACE WOULD TWITCH.

"BUT THE WORST WAS WHEN HE'D TRY TO TEACH ME TO CREATE *ALCHEMITES.*"

LIKE THIS, LACKWIT! REMMEARG IST WITH THE THUMB! IT'S *SIMPLE!*

"ANY WIZARD WORTH HIS SALT CAN CONJURE UP AN *ARMY* OF GLOOMS WITH THE FLICK OF A WRIST.

ME, THE BEST I COULD DO WAS *THESE* FELLOWS.

ISN'T THAT RIGHT, YOU LITTLE WRECKLING?

BUT I'VE NEVER MARRIED, GUMPWORT. I'M THE *LAST* OF THE RUMPLEWHISKERS, SUCH AS I AM.

SO I SUPPOSE WHATEVER YOU WERE *WAITING* FOR, IT NEVER SHOWED UP, EH?

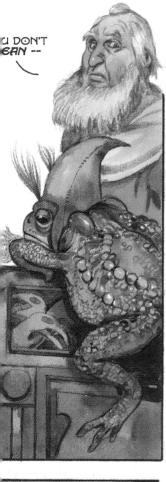

SET YOUR TELESCOPE SO THAT IT CAN SEE THROUGH TIME AND REALITY, NOT JUST SPACE.

Uh, GUMPWORT -- I DON'T REALLY WANT --

AND WHAT WOULD GRIMTHORNE SAY IF HE KNEW YOU HAD THE CHANCE TO FIND THE BOOK AND TURNED IT DOWN?

-SIGH- VERY WELL.

ALL RIGHT. THREE DEGREES UP. TWO OVER. MAGNIFICATION SIX.

TWELVE CENTURIES TO THE LEFT. FOUR REALITIES DOWNWARD. SEVENTEEN MINUTES BACK. NOW -- WHAT DO YOU SEE?

Oh. Oh -- !

"OH, THE *POOR GIRL!*"

HY DID
U *SHOW*
E THIS,
MPWORT?

I'M AN
EVIL WIZARD! A
RUMPLEWHISKER!
A MEMBER OF
THE *DARKSOME
COUNCIL* --

-- EVEN
IF I'M NOT IN
VERY GOOD
STANDING AT
THE
MOMENT.

YOU'RE
FORCING ME
TO GO GET
THE *BOOK.*
WHY?

I *CAN'T
TELL* YOU
THAT.

NOT
YET.

OH,
GUMPWORT.
I
THOUGHT
YOU WERE MY
FRIEND...

hmf?

GO 'WAY...

...LEMME SLEEP...

Ahh! COLD!

ALL RIGHT, ALL RIGHT!

LEAVE OFF, WRECKLINGS! I'M AWAKE!

I HAD THE MOST AWFUL DREAM.

I DREAMED I HAD TO LEAVE THE CASTLE, AND...

OH. RIGHT. I REMEMBER NOW.

IT'S... NICE.

...OOKING IT FROM ...E, I ALWAYS ...GHT IT WAS ... OF GRUBBY. ...ROM DOWN ...RE, IT'S... ...OMEY.

COMFORTABLE.

MAYBE YOU'D LIKE TO LIVE DOWN HERE SOME DAY, BAFFLEROG?

WHAT?

OF COURSE NOT, GUMPWORT. I'M QUITE CONTENT LIVING IN MY ANCESTRAL CASTLE. QUITE CONTENT.

...SE ...RE.

HEIGHDY, STRANGER. WHAT BRINGS YOU TO GRUMBLING?

AND GOOD DAY TO YOU, LAD. I SEEK A HORSE, SUPPLIES, AND LODGINGS FOR MY TOAD HERE.

WELL, BE CAUTIOUS -- THAT'S MY ADVICE! WE GRUMBLERS, WE'RE A SUSPICIOUS LOT! WE HAVE TO BE!

SEE, WE'VE AN EVIL WIZARD NEARBY, WE DO!

WHY, YES, I ...NOW -- IN FACT, ...O HE! BAFFLEROG ...UMPLEWHISKER, AT YOUR SERVICE!

Oh, GO ON -- PULL THE OTHER ONE!

OUR WIZARD'S A FEARSOME MAN, HE IS -- WITH A GREAT BLACK BEARD AND FLASHING CRUEL EYES!

BUT I --

AND WHO MIGHT YOU BE?

HE'S A TOAD, ACTUALLY...

A KING? HOW DOES THAT FOLLOW?

JUST HARKEN TO THE TALE-TELLERS -- *THEY* KNOW.

ALL THE GREAT KINGS OF HISTORY WERE ONCE NO-ACCOUNT THIRD SONS OF WOOD-CUTTERS.

IT'S *TRUE!* KING GWAIN WAS, KING OTTOKAR... KING RUDOLF THE LION WAS EVEN CALLED *"LITTLE DUMLING"* WHEN HE WAS A BOY!

SO YOU SEE, IT'S ONLY A MATTER OF TIME BEFORE I GET *MY* CHANCE. I'LL RESCUE A PRINCESS, MARRY HER --

-- AND THERE YOU ARE, I'M KING. IT'S INEVITABLE!

HMMM. YOU MIGHT LIKE TO KNOW THAT BAFFLEROG HERE IS OFF ON A SECRET QUEST. TO RESCUE THE LOST PRINCESS AND FIND THE *BOOK OF WORSE*...

GUMPWORT, *NO!* DON'T --

REALLY?!

I MEAN -- ARE YOU -- YOU'RE NOT -- *REALLY?*

ABSOLUTELY. MY WORD OF HONOR AS A MAGIC TOAD.

STAY HERE. DON'T MOVE FROM THIS SPOT. I'LL BE *RIGHT BACK,* I PROMISE.

DON'T MOVE!

GUMPWORT, WHAT ARE YOU *DOING* TO ME?

I'VE FOUND YOU TWO HORSES AND PROVISIONS FOR A FORTNIGHT -- GOOD JOURNEY-FOOD, TOO -- AND ONLY *THREE SILVER BITS* THE LOT!

AND MY *MAM* -- SHE'LL TAKE CARE OF THE FROG!

TOAD. AND WHY *TWO* HORSES?

I'M COMING WITH YOU. SEE -- EVEN BROUGHT MY GRAND-DAD'S OLD SWORD!

NO. OUT OF THE QUESTION.

BUT -- THIS IS MY *BIG CHANCE!*

IF YOU'RE GOING ON A QUEST, YOU NEED A SQUIRE -- I CAN DO THAT. I CAN GROOM THE HORSES, GATHER WOOD, MAKE A FIRE -- EVEN COOK!

WELL, I CAN MAKE PORRIDGE. AND IT'S NOT *THAT* BAD...

SORRY. I KNOW YOU MEAN WELL, BUT I'M REALLY NOT UP TO --

HE COULD BE A HELP, BAFFLEROG.

AFTER ALL, YOU'RE NOT A YOUNG MAN ANYMORE.

WELL, COME ON THEN.

IF I'M GOING TO DIE HORRIBLY, I MAY AS WELL HAVE COMPANY.

WHAT IS HE *DOING?*

THOSE ARE PROVISIONS FOR A JOURNEY! AND -- IS HE PAYING THAT WOMAN TO TAKE CARE OF THE *FROG?!*

HE'S FOUND THE BOOK OF WORSE! HE *MUST* HAVE -- IT'S THE ONLY THING THAT WOULD GET HIM OUT OF THAT MISERABLE *CASTLE* OF HIS!

I TOLD HIM -- IF HE FOUND IT, HE WAS TO BRING THE NEWS TO *ME!* HOW *DARE* HE DEFY MY ORDERS?!

IF HE TRIES TO RETRIEVE IT HIMSELF, HE'LL BOTCH THE JOB LIKE SOME LACK-WITTED *APPRENTICE* -- AND THE BOOK WILL BE LOST TO US *FOREVER!*

I WILL NOT *PERMIT IT!*

TO ME, MY GLOOMS!

IT'S GOTTEN AWFULLY DARK...

YES. WE'VE PASSED OUT OF MY REGION BY NOW. THIS IS WHAT MOST OF EVER-NIGHT IS LIKE, ALL THE TIME.

THIS IS WHAT GRUMBLING-BY-THE-SEA SHOULD LOOK LIKE, TOO.

WHAT I'M SUPPOSED TO *MAKE* IT LIKE...

TELL ME THE TRUTH -- YOU'RE NOT A WIZARD AT ALL, ARE YOU? YOU'RE UNDER A SPELL -- OR A HERO IN DISGUISE, RIGHT?

SORRY. IF IT MAKES YOU FEEL BETTER, I'M NOT *MUCH* OF A WIZARD.

BUT -- EVIL WIZARDS DON'T *GO* ON QUESTS. AND THEY DON'T RESCUE PRINCESSES. *DO* THEY?

I DON'T WANT TO TALK ABOUT IT.

ALL RIGHT. YOU'RE JUST -- YOU'RE NOT LIKE I PICTURED AN EVIL WIZARD, THAT'S ALL.

CAN I ASK ANOTHER QUESTION? ABOUT SOMETHING ELSE?

VERY WELL.

WHAT'S *THAT?*

THEY'RE [ST]ORMRAVENS! [THE] SPIES OF THE [AWE]SOME COUNCIL! [TH]EY MUST HAVE [BE]EN SENT OUT [TO] FIND US!

[QU]ICKLY, [BO]Y?! RIDE [FOR] THOSE [H]ILLS!

WHY? CAN'T YOU JUST STRIKE THEM *DEAD* OR SOMETHING?

I'M NOT SCARED TO FIGHT, IF THAT'S --

[N]O, NO -- EVEN IF I [CO]ULD DESTROY THE [ST]ORMRAVENS, THE [MO]MENT THEY SEE US [TH]E COUNCIL WILL [K]NOW WHERE WE *ARE!*

BUT WAIT A MINUTE -- IF YOU'RE AN *EVIL* WIZARD -- THIS COUNCIL -- AREN'T YOU ON *THEIR* SIDE? I THOUGHT --

AK! THEY'VE *SEEN* US!

THEY'LL BE CASTING DOWN LIGHTNING AT ANY MOMENT!

RIDE, RIDE!

...THIS IS WHERE WE WERE HEADED.

HERE? A PITCH-BLACK CAVERN IN THE MIDDLE OF NOWHERE?

YOU KNOW, I HAVEN'T BEEN HERE SINCE I WAS AN APPRENTICE!

IF I REMEMBER RIGHT, WE JUST GO AROUND THIS TURN, AND...

...SEE?

WOW! IT'S *MAGIC*, RIGHT? WHAT IS IT?

THIS IS THE *CAVERN OF FOREVER*. WE CAN REACH ANYWHERE IN TIME, SPACE OR REALITY FROM HERE. THAT'S HOW WE'LL FIND THE PRINCESS.

AND THE *BOOK*, RIGHT?

RIGHT. THE *BOOK*. OF COURSE.

WE'D BETTER GET OUT ONTO THE WATER NOW. IT WON'T TAKE LONG FOR THE COUNCIL TO CATCH UP WITH US.

...NSTERS.
...AN DO
...T. I --

AH!

THERE'S ONE! NOW I'LL --

CHRT?

HUH?

GX!

SIT DOWN, SIT DOWN! DON'T CAPSIZE THE BOAT!

THESE AREN'T MONSTERS -- THEY'RE ALCHEMITES! THEY'RE MINE -- THEY HELP ME!

OH. SORRY.

...MATTER. BUT ...STILL NOW -- ...E GOT TO ...NCENTRATE.

THAT'S RIGHT, LITTLE FELLOW. THAT'S JUST WHAT I NEED! INTO THE BOWL WITH IT.

NO, NOT THE EYE OF --

THAT'S NOT WHAT I --

PUT THAT --

ONE AT A --

NO, YOU --

WRECKLINGS!

STOP HELPING ME!

SO WHAT DID THEY DO? DID THE SPELL WORK? ARE WE GOING TO THE RIGHT PLACE?

I CAN'T BE SURE. I *THINK* WE'LL GET THERE.

I HOPE WE WILL...

KRIK KRA-KABOOM

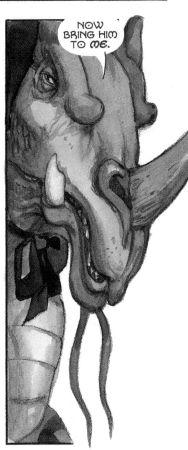

HELLO, GRIMTHORNE.

"-- I HOPE I'VE CHOSEN WELL BY TRUSTING YOU."

SEE ANYTHING?

I'M NOT SURE -- THERE ARE SOME SHAPES UP AHEAD, I THINK.

STILL CHOOSE TO REMAIN SILENT, *TOAD*?

OR WOULD YOU LIKE TO CHANGE YOUR MIND?

OH, BAFFLEROG --

IF IT'S THE PLACE I SAW THROUGH MY TELESCOPE, IT'LL BE A BIG, CONFUSING PLACE, FULL OF PEOPLE AND WAGONS --

-- AND WITH PECULIAR-LOOKING CASTLES BUILT VERY CLOSE TOGETHER.

OH! THE MISTS ARE CLEARING! I CAN --

OH, MY.

OOH. WHAT'S *THAT?*

DAWN. MUST BE DAWN.

THIS USED TO HAPPEN *EVERY MORNING,* BACK HOME.

WOW. MAYBE WHEN WE RESCUE THE PRINCESS, WE CAN MAKE IT LIKE THIS AGAIN?

BAFFLEROG?

AH, HMM. OF COURSE. WHATEVER.

LET'S GO, THEN. IT'S DOWN THIS WAY.

NOK NOK

D, NO, I'M FINE. BUT I ST TELL YOU, PRINCESS -- 5 CAKE IS *DELICIOUS!* VE NEVER TASTED THE LIKE!

Oh, THAT'S SUNSHINE CAKE. GEORGE LIKED IT TOO.

AND PLEASE DO CALL ME *FLORA.*

A CAKE -- MADE OF *SUNSHINE?!*

Oh, DEAR ME NO, THAT'S JUST THE NAME.

IT'S GOT SUGAR, AND EGG WHITE, LEMON PEEL, CREAM OF TARTAR --

IT DOES TASTE LIKE IT, THOUGH, DOESN'T IT?

I SUPPOSE. I'VE NEVER ACTUALLY *SEEN* THE SUN BEFORE TODAY.

Oh, YOU POOR MAN.

Oh, *PLEASE.*

WOULD YOU LIKE TO SEE MY GARDEN?

I'D LOVE TO.

THE *BOOK,* BAFFLEROG -- ASK HER ABOUT THE *BOOK!* IF THERE AREN'T ANY DRAGONS, LET'S JUST DO WHAT WE CAME TO DO AND GO *BACK!*

THAT... WAS A LONG TIME AGO, FLORA.

NEVER AGAIN.

WAS THERE SOMETHING YOU *WANTED*?

OH, NOT MUCH. THERE WAS THIS *BOOK*...

YOU HAD IT WITH YOU WHEN YOU CAME TO THIS WORLD. IT'S NOT IMPORTANT, REALLY.

NOT *IMPORTANT*?!

YOU PROBABLY LOST IT LONG AGO. OR SOLD IT, OR SOMETHING.

I'M SURE IT'S *LONG GONE*...

WHY NO -- I THINK I STILL -- DEAR ME, NOW WHERE -- LET ME THINK --

COME INTO THE HOUSE.

DO FEEL FREE TO COME BACK ANY TIME!
I'VE ENJOYED HAVING YOU BOTH HERE. YOU'RE A VERY NICE MAN, YOU KNOW.

I FEAR NOT.

WHAT'S WRONG? YOU WANTED THE BOOK AND GOT IT, RIGHT? THERE WASN'T ANY DRAGON, BUT YOU GOT IT ANYWAY. AND THE PRINCESS DOESN'T SEEM TO *NEED* RESCUING.

SO -- WE *WON*, RIGHT?

RIGHT?

I DON'T WANT TO TALK ABOUT IT.

3 The Last Evil Wizard

PRINCESS WAS ALL OLD. ~~O~~ DRAGONS. NO ~~SKS~~. NO KNIGHTS ARMORED ALL IN BLACK. DIDN'T EVEN GET TO USE MY GRAND-DAD'S SWORD.

AND YOU STILL HAVEN'T SAID -- -- WHAT ARE YOU GOIN' TO *DO* WITH THAT THERE BOOK NOW YOU'VE GOT IT?

I -- AH --

-- I'VE BEEN ~~T~~RYING NOT TO ~~T~~HINK ABOUT THAT.

AND WHAT IS THERE TO THINK *ABOUT*, BAFFLEROG RUMPLE-WHISKER?

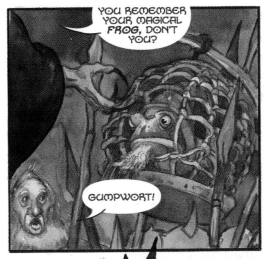

THEY ALL WANT TO BE *PRESENT* WHEN THE MAGIC OF THE DREAD *BOOK OF WORSE* IS *FINALLY UNLEASHED.*

AND WHO CAN BLAME THEM?

I WILL SPEAK THE *ELDRITCH* WORDS THAT CRUSH WHAT *LITTLE* REMAINS OF THE POWER OF *GOOD* --

-- AND OUR LONG-DELAYED TRIUMPH WILL *AT LAST* BE A REALITY!

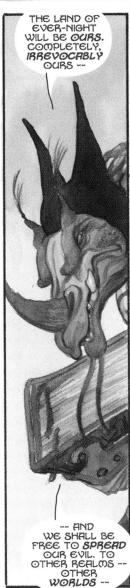

THE LAND OF EVER-NIGHT WILL BE *OURS.* COMPLETELY, *IRREVOCABLY* OURS --

-- AND WE SHALL BE FREE TO *SPREAD* OUR EVIL. TO OTHER REALMS -- OTHER *WORLDS* --

AND TO THINK -- WE OWE IT ALL TO *YOU.*

I NEVER THOUGHT I'D *SAY* THIS, RUMPLE-WHISKER --

-- BUT I MAY JUST BE COMING TO *RESPECT* YOU..!

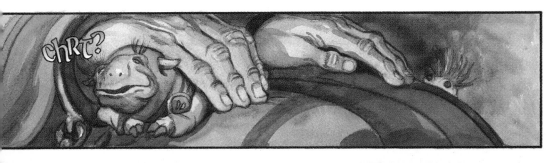

CHRT?

WHAT AM I TO *DO*, LITTLE ONE?

I'M AN *EVIL WIZARD.* RUMPLEWHISKERS HAVE BEEN EVIL WIZARDS FOR AS FAR BACK AS -- AS THERE HAVE *BEEN* RUMPLE-WHISKERS!

IT'S WHAT I *AM.*

I CAN'T DEFY MY *HERITAGE* -- NOT TO MENTION DEFYING THE ENTIRE ASSEMBLED *DARKSOME COUNCIL!*

THEY'D ONLY KILL ME. AND WHAT WOULD *THAT* SOLVE?

OH, WHAT *AM* I TO DO?

CHK TUNK

Eh -- ?

THE COUNCIL AND THEIR CREATURES --

-- THEY'VE BEEN CELEBRATING *ALL THE NIGHT*, AND NOW THEY'RE SNORING LIKE MY *GREAT-AUNT HAGGA!*

AND *WHISHT!* LOOK WHO I *FOUND!*

I *CAN* WALK, YOU KNOW.

YOU'RE *FREE!* THEN YOU MUST *ESCAPE!* FLY FROM HERE AND *SAVE* YOURSELVES! QUICKLY, BEFORE THE WIZARDS *AWAKEN!*

I *CAN'T* DO THAT, BAFFLEROG.

ONE WAY OR THE OTHER, IT ALL *COMES* TO AN END NOW.

YOU DID THIS, GUMPWORT. YOU TOLD ME WHERE THE *BOOK* WAS AND SENT ME OFF TO *GET* IT.

AND WHEN I ASKED YOU WHY YOU GAVE UP YOUR SECRET AFTER SO LONG, YOU WOULDN'T *TELL* ME.

WHY, GUMPWORT?

WHY HAVE YOU *DONE* THIS TO ME?

THE BOOK [C]AN ENSLAVE THE [E]NTIRE LAND TO [EV]IL, TRUE -- BUT [IT] ALSO HAS THE [PO]WER TO SHATTER [EV]IL'S GRIP AND [C]AST IT OUT.

BUT THESE SPELLS CANNOT BE SPOKEN BY A WIZARD OF THE LIGHT. ONLY ONE WHO IS AN EVIL WIZARD HIMSELF CAN DO THAT.

SO THE BOOK WAS HIDDEN -- AND SO I HAVE WAITED. WAITED FOR A WIZARD WHO COULD TURN AGAINST HIS FELLOWS --

BUT I -- I --

YOU'RE NOT ONE OF THEM, BAFFLEROG.

NOT REALLY.

A-AND YOU THINK -- ?

I'M WEAK, GUMPWORT! A WEAK WIZARD, AND WORSE -- A WEAK MAN!

AND -- THERE'S MY FAMILY TO THINK ABOUT -- GENERATIONS OF EVIL TRADITION --

THINK ABOUT ETERNAL NIGHT, OLD FRIEND.

THINK ABOUT YOUR CASTLE -- AND MUDDLE'S VILLAGE.

THINK ABOUT WHAT THEY'LL ENDURE. ABOUT WHAT THEY HAVE ENDURED.

HATCHING SCHEMES WHILE THE WORLD *UMBERS?* I THOUGHT THAT WAS *OUR* SPECIALTY.

Ah, WELL -- NO MATTER.

IT IS TIME FOR THE *CEREMONY.* WE WOULD HAVE SET IT AT *DAWN* -- IF THERE *WAS* A DAWN.

BUT THERE WILL BE NO MORE DAWNS, *WILL* THERE?

TAKE THE FROG *AWAY.*

CHAIN HIM TO THE *ALTAR.* WE'LL BE ALONG DIRECTLY.

THINK ABOUT WHAT I SAID, BAFFLEROG.

THINK ABOUT IT.

SHALL WE?

BUT IT NOT TO BE. ND I ACCEPT MY FATE RACEFULLY.

MAKE THE COUNCIL *PROUD* OF YOU, RUMPLE-WHISKER.

MAKE US ROUD, OR BE SSURED --

-- YOUR DEATH WILL BE *LINGERING AND PAINFUL!*

AFFLEROG -- ?

MUDDLE? BUT HOW -- ?

THE CREATURES -- THEY DON'T CARE ABOUT ONE SUCH AS *ME.* ALL THEY WANT'S *YOU* AN' MAGISTER *GUMPWORT* THERE.

I JUST WANTED YOU TO KNOW -- I *TRUST* YOU, BAFFLEROG.

HE TRUSTS ME! HE *TRUSTS* ME!

WHY COULDN'T I HAVE JUST STAYED AT *HOME?*

DO IT, RUMPLE-WHISKER.

Bightnyng and **fyre**, Ashes and **payne,** You are myne to **commande,** I **calle** on you!

Strike at my --

-- at my enemye --

I CAN'T --

I --

I --

VERY WELL. I'LL CAST YOU A SPELL.

I'LL CAST YOU A SPELL *INDEED!*

-- go aloune!

NO --

-- CAN'T --

OODNESS!

THANK YOU, MY LITTLE FRIENDS! THANK YOU SO *VERY* MUCH!

SO...

NO MORE *DARKSOME COUNCIL.* THEN WHAT...

...WHAT *NOW?*

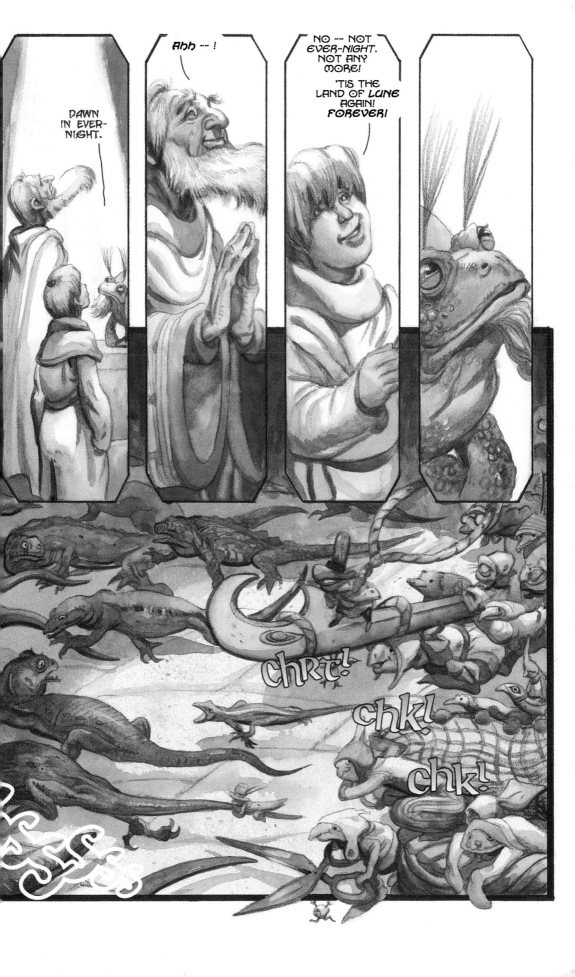

I CAN LIFT THE CURSE NOW, GUMPWORT! I FEEL IT WITHIN ME! I CAN TURN YOU HUMAN AGAIN!

YOU SHALL BE THE *NEW KING* OF THE *LAND OF LUNE!*

AH...THANKS FOR THE OFFER...

...BUT I'D RATHER NOT.

I DON'T UNDERSTAND --

YOU SAVED US ALL! YOU HID THE *BOOK* -- YOU GAVE ME THE STRENGTH TO *RENOUNCE EVIL* --

YES, WELL -- I THINK YOU HAD SOMETHING TO DO WITH THAT YOURSELF.

THE THING IS, I'VE GROWN ACCUSTOMED TO BEING A TOAD. I LIKE IT.

I'D RATHER STAY THIS WAY.

BUT -- WITH THE IRKSOME COUNCIL GONE --

SOMEONE'S GOT TO BRING THE PEOPLE OF LUNE TOGETHER --

TO RE-ESTABLISH *LAW* --

STAVE OFF *WAR* --

YES, LUNE WILL NEED A KING -- AT LEAST FOR THE PRESENT.

WELL, DON'T LOOK AT *ME! I'M* NOT GOING TO DO IT!

IT'S NOT *YOU* I'M THINKING OF.

MUDDLE?

ME -- ?!

WHY NOT? YOU *ACTUALLY* WANT THE JOB.

DON'T YOU?

YES, BUT -- I'M NAUGHT BUT A *BOY* --

YOU SAID IT YOURSELF -- YOU'RE THE THIRD SON OF A WOODCUTTER. IT'S YOUR DESTINY.

BUT I THOUGHT I'D -- I'VE NOT *LEARNED* --

-- I DUNNO HOW TO *DO* IT!

OH, RELAX.

YOU'LL BE SUCCEEDING GRIMTHORNE, AFTER ALL. YOU CAN'T HELP BUT BE AN IMPROVEMENT ON HIM.

UH -- WELL --

-- WOULD THE TWO OF YOU, UM, *HELP* ME, THEN?

BE MY *COURT WIZARDS*, LIKE?

IF YOU LIKE.

ALL RIGHT, THEN.

I'LL BE...

I'LL BE *KING*.

COME FOR THE **CORONATION**, THEN?

AYE...

TRAVELED ALL THE WAY FROM THE WESTLANDS, I HAVE.

ISN'T IT A **WONDERFUL** SIGHT?

THIS IS **RIDICULOUS!**

WHERE'S HE *GOT* TO, THEN?

WELL, HE'S BEEN *TRAVELING* A LOT.

TRAVELING? *BAFFLEROG?* I THOUGHT HE'D GET HOME AND NEVER LEAVE THIS CASTLE *AGAIN!* HE *SAID* AS MUCH OFTEN ENOUGH.

WHERE'D HE TRAVEL *TO?*

WOULD YOU LIKE TO SEE?

HUH? UM -- A'COURSE.

FOLLOW ME, THEN.

Sunshine Sponge Cake

6 egg yolks	1 lemon rind, grated
6 egg whites	1 tsp. almond extract
1 cup sugar	1/3 tsp. cream of tartar
1 cup flour	pinch salt

Sift the flour, measure, then sift four more times. Measure and sift the sugar. Beat yolks with rotary beater until light colored and thick. Gradually beat 1/2 of the sugar and the lemon rind and almond extract into the yolks. Set aside.

Now beat the whites with a wire whisk until frothy. Add cream of tartar. Beat until stiff enough to hold up in peaks, but not dry. Fold in remaining sugar. Cut and fold some of the white mixture into the yolk mixture. Fold and cut in the flour and salt, then the rest of the white mixture.

Place in an ungreased sponge-cake pan (with center tube). Bake 1 hour at 325 degrees. Invert pan; when cool, remove cake.

From The Settlement Cookbook, 1935 edition